His Side of the Story

Z White

BookLeaf
Publishing

India | USA | UK

Presentation by *BookLeaf Publishing*

Web: www.bookleafpub.com

E-mail: info@bookleafpub.com

ISBN: 9789363315150

First edition 2024

This book is dedicated

To: You, the reader! From: Me, the writer!

ACKNOWLEDGEMENT

I would like to thank BookLeaf Publishing & #TheWriteChallenge for their assistance in making these writings become a published possibility! An avenue was provided To: Me, the writer, From: Them, the publisher, for these thoughts, feelings, & ideas to be available to you & that is Absolutely Amazing in itself!

I would also like to thank my friends & family for the support they showed me & my family during one of the most difficult times in our life. There's no way you will ever know how much you all mean to me.

PREFACE

The words you find on the pages of this book were written from the POV of a betrayed partner that was blind sided by news of his partner being unfaithful. After decades of marriage, somehow the door was left open for another man to get in & get to her. He didn't think that was ever even a possibility. The feelings felt & portrayed in this book are real in every sense of the word. What was all this for? At this time, that is still to be determined but one thing is for sure . . . there were lessons learned, prices paid, & memories made.

Why Do I Love You?

I have thought and thought,
I have asked myself at least a million times,
I wanna give a real reason,
Not a fake reason why.

There's a feeling you get when you're with
someone,
It's different than a feeling with just anyone,
It's not because you're beautiful, though you
certainly are,
It's the way you feel gazing at a shooting star.

You make me feel like a real man,
When you say certain things to me,
And I feel like your protector,
Like a hero called Super Z.

You've always had my back,
Through thick and thin,
And you called us a team,
Together we win.

But you can bring me to my knees,
And believe me you have,
No one else has done the things,

You didn't even plan.

But there's something about you,
Different than most,
I've been with you the longest,
No one else ever came close.

10162023

Love During Sex

I won't say I love you when we're having sex,
I will save that for the girl I love.
Sex apparently is just sex to you,
No feelings are involved.

You say everyone loves you when they are fkn
you,
What a thing to say!
There have been two guys in twenty-five years,
And I said it everyday.

So you don't want love during sex,
Well sorry but I do.
So next time we are fkn,
Look me in the eye and say I love you.

10172023

A Single Rose

I'll admit when I first saw you,
It was lust at first sight,
Already had an amazing girl,
But something wasn't right.

Strange how you could make me feel,
Like I was in the wrong arms,
I was already committed,
But hearing some alarms.

The fire started burning hot,
But it was slow and steady,
I didn't pour more gasoline,
'Til I knew you were ready.

But when you finally let me in,
You gave me your all,
It was then I realized,
What it's like to fall.

Celebrated one month,
With just a single rose,
But suddenly I stopped at sixteen,
As the story goes.

If my love was the same,
Then why did I stop?
This could have made her feel,
She was no longer at the top.

One month and two days ago,
You slept in my bed,
I ate you up like the last time,
You gave me amazing head.

Today makes one month,
Since you officially moved back in,
I said I forgive you,
Stay with you until the end.

I hope our love grows in time,
And the trust comes back again,
'Cause the best part of living life,
Is sharing with your best friend.

So where the future takes us,
No one really knows,
But starting today I mark one month,
With just a single rose.

11122023

All Fkd Up

On July nineteenth he went down south,
And that was the first time,
You said 'you got me all fkd up',
Didn't know you would lose your mind.

In April two thousand and twenty three,
There was no other one,
But the devil came and left his mark,
Proud of what he had done.

But he wasn't finished playing games,
He crept into your soul,
And in the spot you held me in your heart,
He tore a tiny hole.

Now I really don't recognize,
The woman that said 'I do',
And I can see that you are starting,
To feel the same way too.

The woman of my dreams,
Who could have such luck,
Now she is no longer mine,
Because she is all fkd up.

12292023

Five Months

Hey fuck face, guess you underestimated love,
You're the kind of person me & her used to make
fun of,

Spitting game with devil's tongue,
Thinkin' all along that you had this thing won,

Now you're back at home living with ma,
Tryin' to figure out how you lost it all,

Here's a news flash it was never yours,
And even though it won't be like it was before,

There's something special about her & Z,
You've had six wives so there's nothing you can
tell me,

Five months ain't shit compared to twenty-five
years,
I ain't talking about the past, the future is clear,

She'll be with me for the rest of her life,
And when you are forgotten, she'll still be my
wife.

16112023

Man To Man

Man to man, I have something to say,
Somehow you got in and stole her away,
It was never gonna work, she was never gonna
stay,
She was just blowing off some steam in the most
fkd up way.

You crept into our lives like a thief in the night,
When she was at her darkest you showed her a
light,
What we have is real and it was air tight,
So there's no way you were taking her without a
fight.

She made her mistake I cannot erase,
But I've also made mine and now I'm on the
case,
Hope I never see you cause I'll put you in your
place,
I'll do a whole lot more than just spit in your
face.

You selfish mfkr, you broke my home,
All you had to do was just leave her alone,

You knew what you were doing, that's why
you're on your own,
Tried to take what was mine and sit on my
throne.

Bitch you could never be me, Alice just fell,
For all your wicked bullshit you had to sneak in
to sell,
Her name is Alice White, not fkn Al,
And I hope sooner than later that you die and
burn in hell.

You said I can have her, she was never yours to
give,
She's not a fkn prize or possession, she's got her
own life to live,
She was devoted to me, the only one she was
with,
But now she's back, she is home, and now I will
forgive.

10182023

White Tank Top

White is the color,
But not always bright,
Every time I see it on,
It always is a good night.

It's shaped just like her body,
With little white lines,
Almost like the 'drive me crazy',
Was made by design.

That little strap that holds it up,
Lays gently on her shoulder,
She was hot twenty years ago,
But even hotter now that she's older.

As it lays across her beautiful breast,
Too tight to leave a ripple,
But God Almighty I Am Done,
When she starts to rub her nipple.

That thing is a fire starter,
Makes every head turn,
You know what they say about fire,
You might just get burned.

Well burn me bitch, fuck me hard,
Let me lick your clit,
Then in return, you can suck my cock,
For just a little bit.

Back to you, I just started,
What is this I see?
Nipple hard as a rock,
And drippin' wet pussy.

I suck your neck, workin' my way down,
Tongue on top of shirt,
And if I lick her pussy right,
I can make her squirt.

When that occurs, I lay her down,
And kiss her once again,
Suck her nipple through her shirt,
Slide two fingers in.

Finger fuck her, suck her titty,
My dick is hard as a rock,
And for some reason, she flips upside down,
Still wantin' to suck my cock.

I let her do what she wants,
And I'm glad that she's with me,
She gets on her hands and knees,
Looks back and says 'Fuck Me Z'.

It's been two hours, I love this bitch,
I don't ever wanna stop,
And all this shit started,
Over a white tank top!

13122023

How To Make It Better

It can never be perfect, it can never be new,
Some would say it's flawed, but I know the real
you.

You're a blank canvas, ready to receive,
And I'm ready to write the future, if you can
believe.

I can believe it, but I've seen it before,
I'll write about sadness, happiness, and much,
much more.

I'll write whatever I want, you deserve a good
story,
'Cause though you've had your own issues,
you've always been there for me.

So who says you're ruined, this is only the
beginning,
See you in fifty years, when I'm closer to my
happy ending.

There will be more tears and a whole lot more
laughter,

So here's to the beginning of our happily ever
after.

Well, I made it to the end and you pulled
through,
I didn't need a new paper, I thought this one
would do.

I'm so happy with what I have, I'm in love and
that's a fact,
And if I need to write some more shit, I'll turn it
over to the back.

10152023

If You Could See What I See

If you could look through my eyes,
At this moment in time,
You would see that God,
Made a perfect design.

Your eyes are the gateway,
Into my heart,
And your body simply,
A pure work of art.

Your skin is so soft,
Like a petal from a rose,
And I love when your nipples,
Pierce through your clothes.

The way that you love me,
Makes me a lucky guy,
I sometimes stare and I'm speechless,
When I look into your eyes.

I could spend every moment,
Being by your side,
And after twenty-five years,
It's still the best ride.

Yea you've made some mistakes,
And I know you regret it,
But you've always been Alice White,
Don't ever fkn forget it.

11022023

Is She Meant To Be Mine?

The girl that I once knew,
Is no longer here,
But was she ever really?
Some things are now clear.

We both made mistakes,
And pain was the result,
Only true love is special,
And it can't be bought.

We paid for our bond,
Throughout all the years,
We had our laughs, made lots of love,
And cried a lot of tears.

So is this love strong enough,
To stand the test of time,
Well it's time that will tell me,
If she's really meant to be mine.

15102023

Two Months

It was two months ago,
When you slipped back in my bed,
Re-consummated our marriage,
Fkd the past out of our heads.

You fkd up, you really fkd up,
But I know I fkd up too,
And out of hurt, anger, and frustration,
We both did what we had to do.

I've been undefeated for a long time,
And I would never let you win,
I was a dickhead and an asshole,
Time and time again.

I know I hurt you, several times,
Over several years,
I know I made you feel unsafe and small,
Made you cry thousands of tears.

I smacked your face, I pulled your hair,
I blamed you a lot,
You then saved up all those tears,
Gave 'em back with just one shot.

Well God has shown us both,
All that we have missed,
Instead of loving unconditionally,
We walk around always pissed.

I love you Alice,
And all your little ways,
I now know you could be gone tomorrow,
So I'll love you just today.

Today is all we ever have,
Things can surely change,
Although it's been twenty-five years,
Suddenly it is strange.

I can't promise twenty more years,
Or even twenty more months with you,
But so far I feel lucky & grateful to have,
At least these last two.

12102023

Tangled Up

Night fall comes
As we sit in amber light,
Her eyes are growing tired,
Sleep she's trying to fight.

As the night passes,
We can feel it getting late,
Soon she'll be all tangled up,
I'll no longer have to wait.

Though we're lying there,
There in the dark,
I know that I am
About to embark.

A night of her skin
Touching my skin,
Every curve of her body,
Yea, it's happening again.

Her sticky sweat
Under my arm,
She is burning hot,
But don't sound the alarm.

'Cause when I touch her,
And then she touches me,
I know that I'm
Right where I need to be.

A cluster of legs
Wrapped up in mine,
She'll be hot as fuck
In a matter of time.

But when we are asleep,
Naked bodies in a spoon,
Arm wrapped around,
Hand cupping her boob.

She reaches up
And grabs my hand,
That kind of shit
Makes me feel like her man.

In these little moments,
Sweaty back to chest,
We melt right into each other,
That's when it is the best.

So if you ask me where is
My favorite place to be,
That's an easy answer,
It's obvious to see.

There are many moments
But I'm mostly thankful of,
The nights I get to spend with her,
Getting all tangled up.

22012024

How Does It End?

As I stroll through this jungle,
That we all call life,
I try to stay busy,
But just think of my wife.

The way we used to be,
Young, innocent, and naive,
Has grown into something,
That's kinda hard to believe.

The towers fell,
But they were rebuilt,
And it's business as usual,
But the sting will always be felt.

They are new and improved,
Stronger than the last,
Been around over twenty years,
But we don't forget the past.

Time can heal wounds,
Love can heal hearts,
But here in this moment,
Is where it all starts.

To escape from my thoughts,
Is all that I'm needing,

Create something positive,
And stop the bleeding.

I'm gonna keep walking this way,
And strive to be a good man,
Question is will I walk alone,
Or will I be holding a hand?

The time is so near,
My heart beats even harder,
I'm scared of what it's like,
Walking around without her.

So on your mark, set, go,
I'm looking around,
Before I step into the future,
My heart starts to pound.

Will you be there?
You're the only one who knows,
You say you gotta plan,
And so the story goes.

Whatever your plan is,
Whatever you do,
Make sure this time,
You do it for you.

01182024

I'll Make It Somehow

I've been walking around,
With my head in a cloud,
Smoking way too much weed,
So that I don't come down.

I was playing around,
Now all I hear are sounds,
Of the rage that's in me,
And I feel like a clown.

I thought I was wise,
What a total surprise,
You could make love to me,
Still look me in my eyes.

You were in disguise,
Now I'm traumatized,
I literally couldn't see,
That you were telling me lies.

But one day I'll look up,
When I fill up my cup,
I'll be living my life,
And I won't give a fuck.

You can say that I'm stuck
Or that I have bad luck,
But when it comes to my wife,
You're just making shit up.

I'm on the corner now,
There's no turning around,
Forward is the only way,
I'll make it somehow.

I'm glad she's around,
Though I hate her ass now,
I love her fucking face,
And we could be love bound.

11062023

Hold My Head Up High

I will hold my head up high,
So that you see my stoicism,
I'll put you back on your pedestal,
Refrain from any criticism.

Consider your opinions,
Be the paper to your thoughts,
We'll remember all the good ones,
And the bad, we'll write them off.

I will speak clearly with my voice,
So you give me respect,
Show no signs of weakness,
But also never neglect.

I will cherish every inch of you,
Especially your heart,
Make you feel like you would die,
If we were ever apart.

I tell you that I love you,
So I'm sure you know,
But you're about to feel it,
Down deep in your soul.

15112023

Who Brought The Pain?
original plus response

This pain that I gain,
Has been etched in my name,
And I won't be the same,
Not sure who's to blame.

I was playing a game,
Not sure who I became,
But I blew out the flame,
And in Satan came.

Ready to take aim,
To a heart with pain,
Got inside her brain,
And then came in the rain.

I'll admit that I'm changed,
This really left a stain,
She got all she could obtain,
And never said a thing.

All I did was complain,
And he was like her cocaine,
She just couldn't refrain,
Now I'm going insane.

11052023 original ^^^

And now my outlook has changed,
Still won't be the same,
This has fkd up my brain,
And brought so much pain.

It brought shame to my name,
I don't like who I became,
Doesn't matter who's to blame,
She still has my last name.

Definitely not the same,
But I am good with the change,
Still feels kind of strange,
But I'm ready to reclaim.

My life with the same,
One beautiful thing,
I'm grateful to obtain,
Alice White is her name.

11122023 response ^^^

Blah Blah Faith

Today I'm feeling blah,
It happens all the time,
So what does that feel like you ask,
Like being left behind.

Like I'm just in a rut,
Running quickly out of luck,
Becoming someone different,
Who just doesn't give a fuck.

What's the definition of trust,
Ever heard of monogamy,
Maybe the only escape,
Is to get a lobotomy.

You see trust out the window,
Loyalty out the window,
Is anything real?
Yeah, but certainly not with him though.

What if temptation comes,
And limerence calls?
Could I be strong,
Or be one of the ones who falls?

I would like to think I would still respect,
My integrity, keep myself in check,
Or do those words mean anything?
Can I have a good wife and still have a fling?

She made some mistakes,
So I know what to do,
But I'm just not sure,
I could follow through.

Guess time will tell,
If I get the chance,
Let's just see,
If I keep my dick in my pants.

13112023

Trapped

I have claustrophobia,
I hate to be tied down,
I hate being in a small room,
With a bunch of people crowded around.

I like knowing certain outcomes,
Surprises make me stress,
I like words like absolute,
Hate words like I guess.

I can deal with a lot of things,
Loyalty is my code,
I like knowing I can trust,
Way on down the road.

I'm not a fan of vagueness,
I need to feel secure,
Nothing else can plague us,
I just need to feel sure.

But lately I've been feeling trapped,
Stuck inside an altered reality,
I'm not sure of who I am or was,
Or even how I'm supposed to be.

All I know is I want out,
Can't stay like this forever,
Feeling trapped inside out,
Wish we were still together.

On the same page,
On the same level,
Now I'm in this fkn cage,
Still fighting with the devil.

So this is my last attempt,
To resuscitate our former selves,
Put our loyalty to the test,
Promise there is nobody else.

And there never, ever will be,
'Til death do us part,
And I no longer feel trapped,
And am no longer in the dark.

17112023

You Were More Than Enough

There used to be a time,
When I was all you ever needed,
But things have really changed,
Ever since you cheated.

Now I wake up every day,
And my brain starts turning,
The thoughts in my mind,
Are constantly burning.

Like who the fuck am I,
If I'm not Alice's man,
Never wondered what that looked like,
Was never part of the plan.

Is this a new beginning?
Is this a brand new start?
Or is it just the biggest test,
To our death do us part?

Can you visualize ten years from now,
But picture me not in it?
Are you living in Alabama?
Have you been there for a minute?

Or did we say fuck the world?
We'll live the best life we can,
Re-dedicate ourselves to each other,
You're my woman, I'll be your man.

This time we go in so much wiser,
Knowing what it takes for success,
The rest of your life with your number one,
Is always the best.

But if the flame has burned out,
And we can't light it back up,
I love you Alice, always will,
You were more than enough.

10022024

Numb

Forty Seven days have passed,
Since my life became undone,
And since the day that she betrayed,
It has been one hundred and one.

I often find myself alone,
In a distant stare,
Thinking about the future,
And if I even care.

The only thing I constantly feel,
Is a high level of grief,
A lot of anxiety,
And a loss in my belief.

It's like I live alone on Mars,
Trying to adapt,
But I've never been to this world,
So I don't know how to act.

All I know is time can heal,
A new life has begun,
I can't wait to live again,
Stop living in the world of numb.

14112023

I Got You!

Young love is amazing,
New love is bliss,
Nothing else matters,
In moments like this.

But true love is rare,
It stands the test of time,
And if you're not aware,
You might get left behind.

You can mow your own grass,
Plant your own seed,
Look over your neighbor's fence,
Man, his grass is so green.

But when you are at home,
You really feel safe,
Your neighbor's on his couch,
Getting shit faced.

'Cause things are amazing,
If you know half the story,
But if the truth could be told,
The life he lives is boring.

A friend for life,
Is what you have in me,
And if things don't work out,
Guess that's how it was meant to be.

I can slowly feel,
You slipping away,
And before you're gone,
I just wanna say.

I will love you forever,
With all of my heart,
One way or another,
It's a brand new start.

So whatever happens,
As a friend or a wife,
I'll always be your,
Ride or die for life.

01202024